Maritta Schwartz

Methods of characterization, character foils (in Jane Austen`s Novels)

GRIN Verlag

Bibliografische Information der Deutschen Nationalbibliothek:

Die Deutsche Bibliothek verzeichnet diese Publikation in der Deutschen National-bibliografie; detaillierte bibliografische Daten sind im Internet über http://dnb.d-nb.de/ abrufbar.

Imprint:

Copyright © 1993 GRIN Verlag GmbH
Druck und Bindung: Books on Demand GmbH, Norderstedt Germany
ISBN: 978-3-640-13132-7

This book at GRIN:

http://www.grin.com/en/e-book/106788/methods-of-characterization-character-foils-in-jane-austen-s-novels

GRIN - Your knowledge has value

Der GRIN Verlag publiziert seit 1998 wissenschaftliche Arbeiten von Studenten, Hochschullehrern und anderen Akademikern als eBook und gedrucktes Buch. Die Verlagswebsite www.grin.com ist die ideale Plattform zur Veröffentlichung von Hausarbeiten, Abschlussarbeiten, wissenschaftlichen Aufsätzen, Dissertationen und Fachbüchern.

Visit us on the internet:

http://www.grin.com/

http://www.facebook.com/grincom

http://www.twitter.com/grin_com

Literatur III: Jane Austen
Dozentin: Dr. Schrick
WS `93/94
Ruhr-Uni-Bochum
Englisches Seminar

Thema des Referates: Methods of characterization, character foils

Maritta Schwartz

1. Plot and Characters

Plot and characters grow together in a perfectly balanced compost of manners and values. Both elements live in the design of manners, customs and values which altogether form the social fabric.

The centre of the novel is the firm and rock-solid society which is based on values like status, manners, education and goodness, which again all rest on wealth.

Those values are absolutes but not constants. This means that a rich man might have a lack of education or goodness and that a poor man might have goodness, education and taste (although this second combination is not very likely).

Of all the values status is the one that comes first. It is sought after by everybody and is displayed to everybody, too. The display is usually also a way of pursuing status, for it indicates what one has a right to covet. The acquisition of status (e.g. inheritance or marriage) is always accompanied by its display.

As status is mainly dependent on wealth, financial prospects are also highly visible in the language that is used in Jane Austen's novels:

a) metaphors of property, money and interest
   time is *divided,* troubles *multiply,* someone is *highly rated*

b) moral interests are put into economic figures
   Mary had no resources for solitude, she had inherited a considerable share of the Elliot self-importance

c) love matters
   declaration, proposal., alliances, prosperous love, to renew an agreement[1]

Financial prospects can be quickly turned into moral vales. An unattainable, wealthy man e.g. is a boor (Darcy), whereas an available man of similar status is considered to be a gentleman (Bingley).

The characters are perfectly woven into the social fabric. While talking to one another, they display formal manners, their mutual bound perspective of social intercourse, their mutual esteem etc. and thereby define themselves and at the same time advance the plot.

The characters always know exactly what they want to say, they truly express and disclose themselves in their talk.[2]

I would like to give two examples for the dependence of character and plot:

1) Lady Catherine de Bourgh tries to force Elizabeth to promise not to engage herself to Darcy. Elizabeth refuses to give any such promise. Later on Lady Catherine informs Darcy about this event and about Elizabeth's behaviour. What she did not know was the fact that she thus encouraged her nephew to propose to Elizabeth a second time.

---

[1] Walcutt, Charles C.; *Man's Changing Mask*, Minneapolis 1966. (S. 72ff.)
[2] ebenda, S. 77f., S. 80.

2) Mr. Bennet is an intelligent, witty and delightful man who tries to avoid the boredom of his wife's and youngest daughter's company. At the same time Mr. Bennet is a prime force in the novel. He is responsible for the disorder in his family, which is due to his withdrawal from them. This withdrawal meant that the education of the children was left to the mother who in turn is not able to cope with this task.[3]

Action and characters art closely connected. It is quite difficult to determine which element is dominant. There is not much action in Jane Austen's novels, but then again people act what they are rather than making crucial decisions to forward the action.

We, for example, never see Lydia actually making the decision to elope with Wickham. From what the reader knows about her before and after the event, she just acted what she was.

Another example would be Jane, who falls in love with Bingley as a course of nature. In the same natural way she bears all the suffers that are connected with it later on. But she never actively does anything to influence the course of action.[4]

2. The different types of characters in Jane Austen's novels

2.1 The three types of 'learning' people

There are three ways of how the heroines in Jane Austen's novels learn about the characters of themselves and the other figures in the novels.

First of all they learn about themselves, partly by self-discovery, partly by enrichment of a relationship.
Then they learn by the discovery of their misjudgements how to achieve a true judgement about those who influence them.
The third way of learning people marks the way in which they register the characters of those for whom they do not deeply care.

The first two methods describe the heroines' experiences of themselves and their lovers. The prime antagonists also belong to the second way of learning. They are subject to the heroines' misjudgements.
The list below gives a short overlook about heroines and antagonists:

Prime antagonists	Heroines	Novel
General Tilney	Catherine Morland	Northanger Abbey
Willoughby	Marianne Dashwood	Sense and Sensibility
Wickham	Elizabeth Bennet	Pride and Prejudice
The Crawfords	Fanny Price	Mansfield Park
Frank Churchill	Emma	Emma
Mr. Elliot	Anne	Persuasion

---

[3] Walcutt, Charles C.; *Man's Changing Mask*, Minneapolis 1966. (S. 85ff.)
[4] ebenda, S. 89f.

The prime antagonists are not necessarily hostile or in opposition to the heroine but they are opposed to the heroine's desires. They are confusing the assumptions, values or principles of the heroine. As a consequence this leads to a frustration of the heroine's growth to self-knowledge (an example would be Frank Churchill and Emma). Another consequence would be the independence of the heroine's fruition of destiny (e.g. the Crawfords and Fanny).

The prime antagonist appears to be dark or confusing to the reader and to the characters in the novel. But the reader gets a clue to a correct judgement that is not necessarily available to the heroine.[5]

2.2 Caricatures

The caricatures belong to the third category of learning people. Their characteristics are of a simple kind. Usually, the do not develop unexpected traits in the course of the story. They are of unaltering distinctness and simplicity.

The list below contains the caricatures in Jane Austen's novels:

Caricatures	Novel
Isabella and John Thorpe	Northanger Abbey
Lucy Steele, John Dashwood, Mrs. Jennings, Robert Ferrars	Sense and Sensibility
Mrs. Bennet, Mary, Kitty, Lydia, Mr. Collins, Lady Catherine de Bourgh	Pride and Prejudice
Mrs. Norris, Lady Bertram, Mr. Rushworth	Mansfield Park
The Eltons, Miss Bates	Emma
Sir Walter Elliot	Persuasion

The caricatures are mostly disagreeable (except Miss Bates). They are invariably comic and more hostile to the heroine than the prime antagonists. The reader as well as the heroine normally are not mistaken about them. An exception is Catherine Morland who does not recognise Isabella's real character first. But this is only an indication for Catherine's stupidity. If the caricatures are hostile towards the heroine, then they are more of a nuisance than a real threat (example: Mrs. Norris in Mansfield Park). The function of the caricatures is to parody or act as foils to the central characters whose qualities are thereby underlined. The caricatures can be a comic exaggeration to the central characters or theca can also function as a contrast to them.

Isabella Thorpe, e.g., with her affliction of friendly devotion and her enthusiasm for romances is the ironic exaggeration of Catherine and her sincere ardours, her naive, romantic indulgences.

Mrs. Norris is an example for a caricature contrasting a main character (Fanny Price). Fanny is a devoted and humble girl, trying to make herself useful. Fanny comes into the house of the Bertrams due to an act of pure benevolence. Later on she becomes part of the

---

[5] Gillie, Christopher; *A Preface to Jane Austen*, London 1974. (S. 104)

family. Mrs. Norris, on the contrary,, creates the illusion of being needed. In the course of the novel this illusion fades away and the Bertrams are glad to get rid of her.[6]

2.3 Minor Characters

In Jane Austen's novels the minor characters remain in the background. They usually have enough life to appear plausible but not too much of it as not to distract attention from the main characters.

Jane Austen is an expert on the art of dimming out characters from the foreground to background. As an example I want to name Mansfield Park. Maria and Julia Bertram are never far from the foreground. The reader is made aware of their self – willed natures, their strong but immature emotions, their competitiveness and mutual jealousy, but still they both do not show real depth of complexity. Behind them, a bit more in the background, we have Mrs. Rushworth, who is an agreeable but slight caricature. Even fainter is Maria's and Julia's brother Tom who is simply the masculine version of their restless superficial energy without any reason for competition and jealousy. Still behind him and even fainter is Mrs. Grant who is described to be endlessly patient with her husband and permanently good – natured.

As the characters recede, they possess fewer and less attention catching fe4atures of temperament, but they seldom fade into total colourlessness.[7]

2.4 Heroines

Jane Austen's heroines possess a fullness of character which grows and unfolds throughout the novel, sometimes into two directions.
The first way is that of critical self – discovery, the second is the slow fruition of innate virtues. Elinor Dashwood and Anne Elliot merely undergo the process of slow fruition. All the other heroines in the novels experience both ways of development.

The ripening of the heroine's virtue always means the ripening of the self, for the heroines do not possess virtues, they *are* the virtues. As the virtues are intrinsic, the ripening sometimes happens involuntarily and the virtues even survive in times of despair. The heroine's virtue is not exhibited for mere public exhibition but communicates itself like a marvellous gift.

There are some basic character traits that all of Jane Austen's heroines have in common. They all accept the limitation of women's scope and all the other limitations people were subject to in those times.
Marriage is the prominent aim of all heroines and they all succeed eventually. Jane Austen's heroines are all in the same state of life. Their hearts are in a state of hope, expectation and competition, when solidarity with other women could be fatal. As society forbids it, the heroines can not openly slide towards their goal (marriage). They therefore develop strategies to reach it: Elizabeth is half – cunning, Fanny is playing the weak, little girl. Jane Austen refuses to glamorize her heroines, none of them is an exceptional beauty.

The same restraints apply to the male characters, too. Henry Tilney and Captain Wentworth show a normal quality of allowable charm. But Edward, Darcy, Edmund and Mr. Knightley are deliberately subdued. On the other hand the charmers (Willoughby,

---

[6] Gillie, Christopher; *A Preface to Jane Austen*, London 1974. (S. 104f.)
[7] ebenda, S. 107

Wickham, Henry Crawford, Frank Churchill) are mercenary, perfidious, unprincipled and mendacious.[8]

2.5 Heroes

The heroes belong to the second category of people the heroines learn about. They influence the heroines but are at the same time subject to their misjudgement because of the complexity of their natures and circumstances. This seems to be quite a plausible thing as young ladies in those times could not meet men in any other way than under the restricted circumstances in society. Therefore, they did not know how men behaved among themselves. Men were some kind of mystery to young women and the more complex their natures were the more mysterious they appeared to be.

Jane Austen's heroes tend to be comparatively unpleasant men although they are never too unpleasant. They just show well concealed traces of arrogance, conceit and recklessness. They teach, humiliate, punish, frustrate and tantalise the women they love, but only to an extent that still allows it to be thought of as an acceptable behaviour. Henry Tilney, for example, is teaching Catherine about the Picturesque, Edmund corrects Fanny's homework, Captain Wentworth lets Anne suffer for more than seven years and Frank Churchill keeps flirting with Emma in the presence of his fiancée Jane. [9]

The heroes are presented to the reader from the heroines' point of view. Therefore the reader only gets an imperfect view of the heroes.

The general task the heroes have to fulfil is that of provoking, offsetting and magnetizing the heroine.
Darcy, for instance, provokes Elizabeth by indifference. Then he offsets her family and environment by his innate fastidiousness and disdain for their provinciality and vulgarity. Later on he goads Elizabeth into rage by his arrogant assumption he would do her some good in proposing to her and thus removing her from her present environment. Furthermore he magnetizes her as a human being as he is capable of feelings that can be hurt.
But not all of the heroes fulfil all those functions. Captain Wentworth, for instance, merely magnetizes Anne and thus restores to her the life of her feelings.[10]

2. 6 Beauty versus Intelligence

Beauty and intelligence – the two elements and their opposition to each other is a constant topic and problem in Austen's novels.

Her novels are full of intelligent men who married beautiful but very stupid women (e.g. Mr. Bennet, Mr. Bertram). The reason is that beauty is the feature that men in the novels consider first. It is not women's mind or character.

Catherine Morland and Fanny Price have to become swans before they are looked at. Anne has to be admired by another man for her beauty to renew Captain Wentworth's interest in her. Sir Walter Elliot is the exaggeration of this regard for mere beauty. Darcy similarly

---

[8] Gillie, Christopher; *A Preface to Jane Austen*, London 1974. (S. 107ff.)

[9] Beer, Patricia; *Reader. I Married Him. A Study of The Women Characters of Jane Austen, Charlotte Brontë, Elizabeth Gaskell and George Eliot*, London 1974.
(S. 68f.)

[10] Gillie, Christopher; *A Preface to Jane Austen*, London 1974. (S. 111ff.)

acts like a judge in a women's beauty contest concerning his attitude towards women (example: walking scene of Miss Bingley and Elizabeth at Netherfield Park).

But in the dialogues Jane Austen makes the men put stronger stress on women's minds. She thus creates a conflict between what she (and her heroines) wishes was true and what is true, a conflict which causes confusion and trouble among her characters.
Captain Wentworth, for example, finds faults in Louisa which he did not see in her during a period of time when she was prettier than Anne. Later on he wants to make Anne believe that he always had valued intelligence higher than beauty (*Persuasion*, chapter 20).[11]

In *Emma* we fin a similar situation. First Mr. Knightley praises intelligence and sense in women and says that Harriet does not possess either of it and that she is merely pretty (p. 48). But later on he praises beauty as the highest possession women could claim. And he tells Emma that it was better for her to be without sense than to misapply it (chapter 8).

Emma has to acknowledge that most men look for beauty in women., although she does not like this idea and would prefer, if they were looking for intelligent women instead.

Knightley later on acts against his own statement (praising intelligence in women) by marrying a silly woman himself – compared to the only reasonable woman in the novel, Jane Fairfax. Jane Fairfax, on the other hand, marries the stupid Frank Churchill.[12]

Sometimes Jane Austen's nervosity about intellect in women is reflected in her heroines. Anne Elliot, e.g., understates her knowledge of the Italian language, when asked to translate a song. Mr. Elliot's reaction shows that she must be a capable scholar of the Italian language (*Persuasion,* chapter 20).
It seems that intellectual qualities in women need male approval to gain some value.[13]

3 General Elements Contributing to Characterization

There are several specific elements and features which serve as means of characterization of the figures in the novels.

3.1 Literature

The view of literature in Jane Austen's novels varies. In general reading is regarded as one of the best ways to improve one's character, but some people do not benefit from it.
The only result that reading has on Mary Bennet, for instance, is that she is annoying her environment with silly quotations all the time.
Sir Walter's favourite book is baronetage. The main pleasure Mary Musgrove gains from books is changing them at the library. On the other hand Captain Harville, who does not read at all, is a very pleasant and amiable man.[14]

---

[11] Beer, Patricia; *Reader. I Married Him. A Study of The Women Characters of Jane Austen, Charlotte Brontë, Elizabeth Gaskell and George Eliot*, London 1974.
(S. 46-48)
[12] ebenda, S. 49f.
[13] ebenda, S. 50f.
[14] Beer, Patricia; *Reader. I Married Him. A Study of The Women Characters of Jane Austen, Charlotte Brontë, Elizabeth Gaskell and George Eliot*, London 1974.
(S. 51f.)

Literature can even occur as a harmful factor. In *Northanger Abbey* the lecture of Gothic novels affects Catherine Morland's judgement on reality. In *Sense and Sensibility* Marianne Dashwood learns from poets to cultivate the role of the girl with the broken heart. In *Mansfield Park* the characters confuse their already confused feelings and relationships by acting a play that parodies their own lives.

Jane Austen makes particularly fun of people reading poetry. Anne's view of poetry is presented in these sentences:

> "She thought is was the misfortune of poetry to be seldom safely enjoyed by those who enjoy it completely; and that the strong feelings which alone could estimate it truly were the very feelings which ought to taste it but sparely."

(Persuasion, chapter 11)

Accordingly the excessive consume of poetry is considered to make men womanish (or: only womanish men can read an excessive amount of poetry). This view is manifested in Admiral Croft's remark that *"James Benwick is rather too piano"* for him.[15]

3.2 Flirtation

Many of Jane Austen's heroines are flirtatious. But they are not designing coquettes. They always say what they mean and mean what they say. So a *"yes"* means *"yes"* and a *"no"* means *"no"*.[16]

3.3 Dresses

The heroines have no taste for finery or parade. The heroines do care about their appearance, they always look charming and appropriate. Their dresses are tasteful but simple.

3.4 Marriage

Marriage is the heroines' prime object, but they never panic about it. The financial improvement of a marriage retreats behind affection.
Jane, for instance, grieves for Bingley, when she has to think that he has lost his interest in her. She does not grieve for the status that he could have offered to her. Elizabeth's reaction is similar, when she cannot hope for a second proposal of Darcy.
Emma pretends not to see any need of a marriage because she is rich (but later on she becomes aware of her love for Knightley).
Lady Russell is rich and does not desire men (= sex) anymore.[17]

3.5 Proposals

Marriage proposals are left to men, entirely. But, nevertheless, young women are allowed to encourage men.

---

[15] ebenda, S. 54f.
[16] Beer, Patricia; *Reader. I Married Him. A Study of The Women Characters of Jane Austen, Charlotte Brontë, Elizabeth Gaskell and George Eliot*, London 1974.
(S. 56)
[17] ebenda, S. 60f.

Elizabeth, e.g., tries to encourage Darcy by her emotional outburst of gratitude because of his great help in the arrangement of Lydia's marriage with Wickham.

Anne's tactic is different. She speaks aloud to Captain Harville about women's (and, of course, her own) feelings.[18]

3.6 Accomplishments

In Jane Austen's novels, women's accomplishments do not play a great role. The heroines are often rather indifferent performers, but they do not mind performing. Elizabeth, e.g., does not play the piano very well. But the men who are in love with the heroines do not mind those deficiencies.

3.7 Music

Music reflects the sexual status of women: the performance of music is a task that is left mainly to unmarried women. Married women often do not give performances anymore.[19]

3.8 Shooting and Hunting

These activities are masculine accomplishments with an important symbolic meaning: They symbolize men's *hunt* for a wife.

But shooting and hunting can also be hobbies of dissatisfied or unhappily married men (e.g. Willoughby, Charles Musgrove).

3.9 Driving

Driving is also a masculine accomplishment. Men exploit the possession and the skill of handling a carriage to impress women. Men fancy themselves as drivers and girls can sort them out by this criterion.

Sitting beside the driver is of special importance for young women as it is a sexual achievement. Mrs. Grant, for example, wants Julia to sit next to Crawford. This is an expression of her wish for a marriage of the two.[20]

3.10 Friendship of Women

There seems to be no really deep relationship and friendship possible among Jane Austen's women. They consistently tend to throw each other to the wolves. An example would be Mary Crawford, who is not on Fanny's side, when Henry announces that he wants to make Fanny fall in love with him.

---

[18] ebenda, S. 61ff.

[19] ebenda, S. 64f.

[20] Beer, Patricia; *Reader. I Married Him. A Study of The Women Characters of Jane Austen, Charlotte Brontë, Elizabeth Gaskell and George Eliot*, London 1974.
(S. 74ff.)

3.11 Friendship of Men

There does not seem to be much solidarity among men, either. This can be seen even in the relationship between Darcy and Bingley which appear to be quite intimate at first sight. But Darcy dominates Bingley and manipulates him in his feelings for Jane.[21]

---

[21] ebenda, S. 76f.

4 Bibliography

Austen, Jane; *Emma*, Penguin Classics, London 1985.
        – *Mansfield Park*, Penguin Classics, London 1985.
        – *Northanger Abbey*, Penguin Classics, London 1985.
        – *Persuasion*, Penguin Classics, London 1985.
        – *Pride And Prejudice*, Penguin Classics, London 1985.
        – *Sense & Sensibility*, Everyman, London 1978.

Beer, Patricia; *Reader. I Married Him. A Study of The Women Characters of Jane Austen, Charlotte Brontë, Elizabeth Gaskell and George Eliot*, London 1974.

Gillie, Christopher; *A Preface to Jane Austen*, London 1974.

Walcutt, Charles C.; *Man's Changing Mask*, Minneapolis 1966.